THE MORNING NEWS
IS EXCITING

ACTION BOOKS

Editors JOYELLE MCSWEENEY & JOHANNES GÖRANSSON

Art Directors ELI QUEEN & JESPER GÖRANSSON

Web Editors JOHN DERMOT WOODS & EMILY HUNT

Editorial Assistant KIMBERLY KOGA

Graphic Designer ROBERT McKENNA

Action Books gratefully acknowledges the generous support of the College of Arts and Letters at the University of Notre Dame.

Action Books

356 O'Shaughnessy Hall

Notre Dame, IN 46556

www.actionbooks.org

The Morning News Is Exciting

ISBN: 978-0-9799755-6-1

Library of Congress Control Number: 209944060

First Edition

Table of Contents

· ·

MANEGG

1 SAY NO LAME!
....

Say no lame! Say we care. Terror can't tell
and bears a crown in the kitchen, may we?
Who cares: cunt can't battle, key won't tear.
Ugly decay, care for Pa and tell, we lonely.
So jail men care, met a lavish man, met a landlord.
(Eggpisode loiter ha! Advance don't at all, assuming mellow)

Me, countless, out to tear. Sane no, lend me.
Say I can't rain, end me.

At least sit well, we command:
Men say he but tally saying no, lame!
Who can respond. None say none! My wind, way low.
Lie, Egg, more lonely and bare, a callous lock.
Truly true Lass pause and care.

Allow oat to chant:
Let me say align, align,
Titan of Adam, you seem dense.
Let me say in-law, in-law
I won't lay an eggy egg.

2 SAY YOU LESS

Say you less, lay.

Let's say we yoke you.

You wrote: lard land more, you're ever less, weep for you.

Epi-sale and jot well, lame.

Leave! Let's land, she's none, a lone planet.

Come, have a long life and then glow-glow.

Leave!

Delete you last.

Kick her trimming.

Kick her trimming.

You,

die you!

Some land more. None land far.

Pa, you kill none, paw-paw.

Tad late, sit and read.

Tad late, doubt what you've read and ban joints of cliché.

Robin's yokelet glossary aka cover Ma's envy.

Epi and phony, view well, limber.

Solely in case, mate more so.

And then hatch later, event very parent.

Come and lay me low.

See your coop jingle and then accept sherry.

Leave! Who cares: bake her.

Who cares: natal and body, *discipline is an art of rank.*

Who cares: care free epi-power, *it is a type of power.*

Who cares: a blasé son brags, *a technique.*

3 NONE SAY NONE
....

None say dumb, none say none.
Yoke behind and be fair, only to piss on.

Call Ma, arrive as we care to come and watch you comb.
Save and grin, wee and we, Hen revolts and bets on awe.
Ravine lone mankind, ravine luscious sex.

Duet in-law chills and then blames flan.
He's dirty, lays share and then cares drawl surface.

Beware-beware girl, might and navel can fray.
Mate and then sing, fate and then fake.
Read louder, only the gruel lacks and swells.
Let me think, say grinning could only cap our way.

Pie pie rye beyond your sale: what do man and planet doubt about?
Fly beyond and land more: domain plan is forgot about.

Fuckingness and then sexy do agree.
Met a jerk and then laid a proper yoke.
Call Ma, *discipline organizes an analytical space.*
Say we, find an epi-norm, land more, tally more?

4 I SAID TO ME

Me, me, river.

Then Egg, I taught: the key to baggage is tot and tot

and *the disciplinary space is always, basically, cellular.*

Send mass, send lard, send game, end, let go.

Same, lay me there, I said to me.

Revel in bland night and permit joy, boy.

How can I say for we?

      Sac à la King, really, add pinch of salt.

      Carry your noun pre-dead!

5 SAC À LA, REALLY

Sac à la, Really, none say none.

Egg-nagged Pa repented: Say very, none say dumb!

Ailing Pa cannot pee, pie pass for all, care for cheese?

Really! Really! land more!

Very!

Sac à la King feigning contract, rat trap!

Really! Really! land more!

Beyond day, not yet. Say more aka partly combed Lad

Yes, Pa. Retake mothball. Really. Day more, die more.

Really! Really! land more!

Very!

Sac à la King feigning contract, rat trap!

Really! Really! land more!

6 AH! PIE
. . . .

Ah! Pie tall and wit-late. Epi-pep, sit well

like Pie, taste and count languid-land.

Lay, care, locate, possess and then

care about land-me, why?

Midday! I solely laid beyond nit for jerk!

Midday! I then read to achieve wifely.

I name lame, kind and lame, recite to fetal bland Man.

Boy. I grin and care, clean later,

recite size to him: The Lonely and the Restless.

(I lament solely coyly to universe and you.)

Say now, say this is a noun for Pa, none Man?

7 OH TIZZY
....

Oh tizzy of tame-boy, do vent joy,

oh tizzy come and land more, oh tizzy convey

none on land...?

Oh tizzy rain more, oh tizzy make man thought,

oh tizzy same thought,

oh tizzy lay off thought, oh tizzy layaway thought...?

—I say sac, I mourn, taught by govern and lay.

I say layout the treatise!—

Kind of lone-man? Kind of late sing-along?

> *Chuck baggage merrily*
>
> *Chuck baggage and then miss you*

I solely lay beyond nit for jerk.

Notes on MANEGG

. . . .

Manegg is a homophonic translation of *Manteg* by Monchoachi in *Cahier de poésie*, (Paris: Gallimard, 1980).

Italics: Michel Foucault, *Discipline & Punish: The Birth of the Prison*, trans. Alan Sheridan (New York: Vintage Books, 1995).

DIARY OF RETURN

8 AUG 2002
. . . .

I arrived below the 38th parallel. Everyone and every place I know are below the waist of a nation. Before I arrived, empire arrived, that is to say empire is great. I follow its geography. From a distance the waist below looks like any other small rural village of winding alleys and traditional tile-roofed houses surrounded by rice paddies, vegetable fields, and mountains. It reminded me of home, that is to say this is my home.

Close up: clubs, restaurants, souvenir and clothing stores with signs in English, that is to say English has arrived before me and was here even before I had left. PAPA SAN, LOVE SHOP, POP'S, GOLDEN TAILOR, PAWN. I followed the signs and they led to one of the gates to Camp Stanley, a heliport, that is to say *language is not to be believed but to be obeyed, and to compel obedience.* A woman in her seventies lived next to LOVE SHOP. She was taking an afternoon nap. She has never left below the waist and eventually came to be regarded as a great patriot by her government, that is to say she followed the signs and suffered from lice infestation during the war and passed the lice on to the GIs. I followed the houses that reminded me of home. They led me to another metal gate and barbed wire. Another woman was having lunch at My Sister's Place. She did not remember which year she had returned except that she remembered hearing about the assassination of our Father, that is to say she was here and I was still elsewhere and *the unity of language is fundamentally political*. She told me a story with her right index finger. Her finger fiercely pointed to her mouth, then between her spread legs, and then her behind. She had no choice under the GI's gun, that is to say she had no choice about absolute choice, that is to say her poverty was without choice and when absolute choice was forced upon her she chose a GI, that is to say she chose empire because empire is greater than our Father, that is to say she followed and left her daughter to its geography and her index finger had no choice but be fierce under absolute choice, that is to say she had arrived home.

28 OCT 1992
....

Yun Kŭm-i's head was smashed with a Coca-Cola bottle. She was found dead, legs spread with the Cola bottle in her vagina and an umbrella up her anus. That is not to say empire does not endorse one planet or Father's umbrella. On the contrary, it enforces *grammaticality* within and without before and after Father sprinkles white disinfectant powder on the index finger. *No one is supposed to be ignorant of grammaticality.*

10 SEPT 1999

Another mysterious death of a GI's woman.

She had bled profusely and dark spots were found all over her body. Her face was flat against the floor with her tongue protruding. Her landlady called the police because she hadn't seen her tenant for several days. What kind of work did she do?

She stopped working at a club in hopes of starting a new life. That is not to say GIs will now rape any women due to homesickness and R & R. What needs to be said is that from elsewhere I translate the report of the death of a woman I met two months prior in Tongduch'ŏn and that colonial distance can be saturated with separation due to homesickness of a different nature. That is not to say there isn't resistant bilingualism, as opposed to colonial bilingualism, predicated on oil and formaldehyde flowing as one river below the waist from empire's base, but that *there is no mother tongue, only a power takeover by a dominant language.* Then translation for me is a form of exile and empire. Are & I.

10
. . . .

When I return when I return I say things are near of a nearness when I say such things as the little soldiers are napping after lunch inside a bus with barred windows in front of the city hall. I say things are near of a nearness when I say empire's embassy is practically next door, guarded by the napping soldiers. When I return when I return all grown up and bigger than the napping soldiers I say things are small of a smallness the dearness of it all. When I return when I return I look up at the TV screens above Father's plaza where sons of sons cheered a game of soccer for Father even when empire's embassy was practically next door. Knock on the door, kneel on the ground and fill out the application which happens to be no more since Father's children have finally made it to the waived visa list. When I return when I return I say my twin of a twoness paces the bridge over the river of oneness and translates exile of an exileness and empire of an empireness while I trace the alleys of my childhood and find no one. When I return when I return all grown up and bigger than the napping soldiers I say near of a nearness when I say Russian women take their daily stroll at night along the forest path behind empire's heliport and Filipino women with toddlers in broad daylight walk down the strip of clubs of clubs called a SHOPPING MALL because *all signs are signs of signs.*

This is our perspective regarding the death of a woman in Itaewon. Ms. Kim, 32 years old, was found on the floor with blood all over her naked body at NEW AMAZON, an American military personnel-only club. Ms. Kim died soon after she was taken to the hospital. GI Christopher McCarthy was arrested on February 21 for the murder of Ms. Kim. He confessed that he had beat and strangled Ms. Kim when she refused to comply with his demands for unusual sexual acts. *What is called style can be the most natural thing in the world; it is nothing other than the procedure of a continuous variation. Because a style is not an individual psychological creation but an assemblage of enunciation, it unavoidably produces a language within a language.* This is our position regarding the death of Sŏ Kyŏng-man in Kosan district of Ŭijŏngbu. The 66 year-old woman was found dead on the floor drenched in blood. Her landlady found her at approximately 2:20 PM. Ms. Sŏ had bruises around her eyes and her two front teeth were knocked out. According to the witness, she was seen entering her room with a GI the night before around 11:50 PM, and soon after a fight broke out. As a child Ms. Sŏ suffered an illness that left her deaf and mute and she had to fend for herself after she was separated from her family during the war. *Actually, there is no question, answers are all one ever answers. One should bring forth the order-word of the order-word*: sons of sons, clubs of clubs. *In the order-word, life must answer the answer of death.* There are pass-words beneath order-words: farewell of farewell, return of return.

Italics: Gilles Deleuze and Felix Guattari, *A Thousand Plateaus: Capitalism and Schizophrenia*, trans. Brian Massumi (Minneapolis & London: University of Minnesota Press, 1987).

THE MORNING NEWS
IS EXCITING

TO ALL BOYS AND MEN!

Dandelions may not be weeds. They are related to chrysanthemums. Girls should.

May all weeds dislocate themselves. Girls should. I clench my fist and watch the morning news. Dandelion leaves are bitter yet tender. Girls should. Chrysanthemums are admired. Beware. The early morning news is exciting.

SPECIAL ATTACHMENT

I take a long shower. Girls should. I have suffered. I have been mistaken. Doctors and nurses know absolutely nothing. I despise them. They know absolutely nothing. I know everything that will happen. I enrage the world. Girls should. My dishes are unbreakable.

EXCEPTIONAL ATTACHMENT

Squeeze plenty. Girls should. Wash and wash then write to the world. The news will break. Just wait and see. I have all the kitchenware. Just bring your clothes. Girls should. I write to the world. My book is taped up in a box. Wash and wash till the smell is gone, blood is gone. I am most bored in the morning.

MORE ON ATTACHMENT

Everyone is born wanted or unwanted, but some may be born exceptionally unwanted or wanted. A nation may be wanted or unwanted depending on what the other nation is thinking about. This nation was exceptionally wanted then unwanted because it was thought to be precariously small. Whatever happens to this nation will be revealed gradually even though the morning news is exciting. Fathers, sons, boys are usually exceptionally wanted. At times they can be born exceptionally wanted then unwanted because they are thought to be precariously secondary. This father was precariously secondary. He knew this nation well but he knew the other nation even better. This is what happens when the other nation thinks a lot about a nation and stays an unwelcome stay. There is another nation that thinks about this nation but whatever is to happen will be revealed gradually despite the fact that the morning news is exciting. This father who was secondary amongst wanted existence had sadness about unwanted existence. Nevertheless this father took pictures of this nation before, during, and after the war.

A BLUE SUITCASE

Twin twin twin zone. Cameraman, run to my twin twin zone. A girl's exile excels beyond excess. Essence excels exile. Something happens to the wanted girl. Nothing happens to the unwanted girl. The morning news is exciting. Excessive exile exceeds analysis. Psychosis my psychosis. Psychosis her psychosis. Pill her and pill her and file her and exile her and pill her and pill her till axis and boxes and sexes.

LET'S GET LOUD
. . . .

STUDENT REVOLUTION = APRIL 19, 1960, SOUTH KOREA

S = SEX = FILE = EASY

R = REPEAT = PETITE

A = ASS = ASK

19 = CENTRAL = COCK = MAN

1960 = WANTED = SOMETHING

S = SOUTH = WORLD

K = KOREA = WORLD = DEAR NATION

It is easy to tell the uniformed students are following and something is blazing. On the other hand the morning news is exciting. Of course near narration is exciting. Cameraman, run with the shoeshine boys and watch them die. They made themselves into a single mass by locking their arms and shoulders and moving like a tide. Hence bring down the world. Whereas the elite was petite the center was cocky and manly. As you can see dear nation was petite and wanted.

Hence dear narration. Watch me shine.

NOTHING HAPPENS
....

I have written LETTERS. I sat in my car and cried for a long time.
Then I lashed out. I decided to write a long letter. When nothing hap-
pens I cannot repress my rage. Far nation calls you and you go. You
run with a camera. Far nation pays you to run. Hence morning news
is exciting. Far nation pays the petite nation to run. Naturally you
run and follow the bomber. You sit behind the electronic warfare of-
ficer and puke. Manage your fear, far narration is here. Everyday life
seen through everyday eyes. Troops on foot. Flashes of napalm in-
tercut with everyday man singing and playing a guitar. Flashback to
Ho. Everyday woman and infant looking distressed. Everyday man's
guitar. POV from F-4. Very low level. Series of aerials looking back
over everyday craters. Glistening water. Aerial nation for everyday
eyes. Hence I wait for the morning news. She has written that noth-
ing happens to the unwanted girl. What error. She's an errorist.

NOTES OF A COWRY GIRL

1

I am a cowry girl, a marine biologist to be exact. In 1930, Queensland, the shells were found. White, so pale, no pattern, one shell. White but markings. One shell. Overlaid by three shells. Normal. One shell. Other shells were unspotted. Color photographs were taken by Mr. Goadby. They showed no difference. All were colorless and transparent, with about 100 rows of teeth. No difference. Two forms occasionally imperfectly omitted. Therefore be considered a synonym.

Has anyone personally found living or dead specimens outside of this area? The editor. Mr. Goadby. As discussed elsewhere. Proposed to rename. Split it into two. The second being. The evidence is against the second. Therefore be considered a synonym.

Mr. Goadby: There is a good case to be made for the original name. Therefore be considered a synonym. A pair found under a stone. Unfortunately, the holotype is the single. The time of publication of the original. It will settle any future dispute. Identification. Other kinds of types. They will be discussed.

Teeth. It is obviously not possible to compare directly. Therefore be considered a synonym. A formula for converting all teeth. All other teeth counts. The formula is: reduced number of teeth. Whenever this method is used, teeth will be described as "reduced." As time goes by the editor will write less and less, and I will write more and more.

2

I am a cowry girl, a marine biologist to be exact. The 8-hour movement started in the United States in 1884. Feeling more and more. Gave birth. Took up the question. 8 hours shall be the norm. Marx: Slavery disfigured a part of the republic. Labor with a white skin cannot emancipate itself where labor with a black skin is branded. The time named. Endorse the same. Half of the same. More profoundly. Therefore be considered a synonym.

Although nothing was said, feeling more and more. Gave birth. Science, however, makes progress even in times of war and other troubles. Unusual forms were named in cases where the difference could have been due to environment and not to genetics. Strikes during. Strike movement. Sympathetic strikes. Sympathetic norms. The enemies of the workers, however, did not remain idle. Bourgeois historians speak of the "social war" and "hatred for capital." Feeling more and more. Please—not to the bank.

Engels: As I write these lines. The spectacle we are now witnessing. The determined will of the working class to destroy class distinctions. Thus enter on the road. If only Marx were with me. May Day became Red Day. Therefore be considered a synonym. In September Mr. Goadby is going to live in Australia, and will continue distribution of "The Cowry" from there. As time goes by I will leave here and go there.

3

I am a cowry girl, a marine biologist to be exact. Memos blur beyond the pale. Cruelty wasn't cruelty. A certain amount of violence does not exceed the norm. Since the 18th century, "cruel" and "unusual" have been coupled. Therefore be considered a synonym. Vexed by ambiguity. Guantanamo and elsewhere. The blurring of distinctions. Differing chiefly by reduction.

Remove the animal. If you are going to sacrifice the shell, cut it with a hacksaw from end to end. Defense: My impression. I believe. Technically is different. Imperfectly omitted. In other words, what mattered in the American context was unusual cruelty in method of punishment, not the prohibition of excessive punishments. Repeat the procedure. If the animal has dried in the shell, soak the shell in water for a day before removing. The teeth face up. Move gently to and fro. Please—not to the bank.

Ten lashes. For not picking enough cotton or leaving cucumbers on the vine. Goodell: The masters and overseers have only to repeat. Hollow pretense. Press it gently down. The film of mounting. Not in the editor's collection! Teeth at top and bottom. The repetitiveness and doubletalk. Therefore be considered a synonym.

The formula is: reduced. On June 10, 2006, three detainees at Guantanamo committed suicide. An act of asymmetrical warfare. Some shells are completely white. The technique needs practice. A table for easy conversion will be given. Lastly, don't despair if things go wrong.

Notes on NOTES OF A COWRY GIRL

Texts from: *The Cowry*, Vol. 1. No. 2, edited by Lt.-Col. R. J. Griffiths (1961).

History of May Day by Alexander Trachtenberg (International Publishers Co. Inc., 1977. First published in 1929).

The Story of Cruel and Unusual by Colin Dayan and foreword by Jeremy Waldron (A Boston Review Book, The MIT Press, 2007).

INSTRUCTIONS FROM THE INNER ROOM

1

Females are silent

Add plenty of detergent

Emerge like a nation

Sing as if you are male

Your abdomen is hollow

Call him and call him

like a speaker on high volume

Females are silent

Set the water high and

rise behind the loneliest trees

Tell him you're here

Claim his wig—it's yellow

Glow as if you care

Expose his shit right away

Peel his moon if you dare

2

Place a kitchen knife deep

inside the washer

Drain water and soap

Your arms ail

At the end of the spin

stay cool, stay mute

Answer the door

Answer the nation

It's yours, it's mine

It's him Yellow Hair

A brief chat

Unload your load

Bang him against the dryer

Make a wig of him then propose

Let his hair grow inside you

Wash it daily with your heart

3

Life begins now

Have no doubt

Have no door

This is not your fault

Run the rinse cycle twice

Don't let the bubbles flow over

Life begins now

Have no doubt

Tea and Language

They say it's a sensation

Why pee like a nation?

On the domestic front a quiet revolution is taking place

Son of a nation—nation's son

It's an issue, tear a tissue – the Tissue Door –

Use it to lift the cover

Rip another for your ass

Drop it into the bowl

Pee before it sticks to the bottom

Father is supreme

Your urine is serene

Turn around

Did you flush? Flush

4

Marry soon

Marry, marry again

Wait and wait, late, late

Marry him, him

My mate, marry

Marry your knuckles

Hierarchy—it's expensive

You want to die

for you are pensive

In forest, you want to die

In valley, you want to die

You want to die, boulders, fir

Alone, you want to die

Peel the detergent box

Blood carries dormant cysts

Did you rinse the cutting board?

Do it again, did you?

Do it again do it

Did you?

5

Hence, a son of a nation is a son of a butcher

he hooks cow's butt, he hooks

he hooks cow's neck, he hooks

he hooks cow's nose, he hooks

he hooks cow's ears, he hooks

he hooks cow's feet, he hooks

he hooks cow's lips, he hooks

he hooks cow's fat, he hooks

6

I have one more thing to tell you

Don't envy another's wealth

Don't be negligent of nation

Concentrate on house management

Pack bags, pack eggs

pack pegs, pack pigs

It's done, well done

Your in-laws will smile

Sit for a while

Your husband is the sky

He'll land one day

Act in a timely manner

Explain to him in an orderly fashion your zeal

Stand up appropriately when you leave

You are peeved

Pack up, pack north

pack down, pack south

Remove your seal and beg

Your husband is the sky

He'll land one day

Open his seam then close

Open again

Notes on INSTRUCTIONS

In pre-modern Korea, self-educated, upper-class women wrote in-structional poem-songs (*kyubang kasa*) that were mainly passed down from woman to woman, mother to daughter. These poems, usually recorded in vernacular Korean, *hangŭl*, spoke of family ge-nealogy, proper conduct, duty and obedience to husbands, in-laws, and parents.

THE TOWER

No one spoke to her
but she married anyway.
She loved her bedroom, her tower.
She slept alone on a mattress
covered in Ziploc garbage bags.
Her blue suitcase was packed
and ready to go.

At her wedding, she'd stayed
solemn behind her veil.
She gave her husband a ring
then let go of his hand.
Still no one spoke to her, so
she sat next to a photographer
and drank her champagne.
Later she entered a toilet stall
and watched the water swirl,
go down, then come up again.

She preferred her bedroom
where she could lament alone
and wipe the dust off her blue suitcase.
Her husband was normal and distant.
Goodhearted, he liked to fuck.

No one speaks to me, she told him.
Then she went into her bedroom
and locked her dress, her door.

That night she laughed while
straightening the garbage bags
on her mattress. She knew joy,
she knew Freud. She thought
her hands were sleeping. They
touched neither man nor woman.

She asked *OED* for power.
Tower is power. She preferred power.

Her sleeping hands slept in the forest.
All was neglected, all was selected.
Her unconscious was common to all:

We sleep, we are.
All neglected, all selected.
Natural, national selection.
We belong and long
for the supernational.
There is no comparison.

Plastic, of course.

Transparent act, you rock.

Bag it, dust, dust, bag

without garb.

Come in. Come in. Have a cigar.

She went in.

Has anyone read

Spectral Nationality:

Passages

Of Freedom

From Kant To

Postcolonial

Literatures

Of Liberation?

You are not asleep.

Fine, fine. Sit down.

She sat down.

Here, need a light?

You know, gladiolas can live.

To hell with the swans.

How to decolonize.

My forest, my ass.

Where were you prior to the Fifth Republic?

I frequented The China Emporium.

Everything was cheap there.

Not Chinese, not British

no one spoke to me.

I bought silk blouses bagged in plastic.

I thought supply, supply.

Are the workers communists?

Am I asleep? Do I supply?

I was to marry someday in a forest.

Elevators quickly filled with yellow heads.

Smell of milk nauseated me.

What was I to do?

Zipbloc bags came in handy.

Try bagging soy.

After my shower, I pulled out hair from the drain.

They say unwilling departure leads to exile.

In brief, she is lost inside the Emporium.

She prefers power.

She suffers from neglected supply.

An embroidered tablecloth and

Mao's Little Red Book.

Loss is gloss as she navigates the sea of empire.

She dreams of the return and national conclusion.

She is obsessive to the end.

She protests on the platform of ceremony.

Loss is gloss as she navigates the entire hegemony.

Ziploc bags come in handy.

She tears the bag and gags.

It is the only way.

Notes on THE TOWER

. . . .

Italics: Pheng Cheah, *Spectral Nationality: Passages of Freedom From Kant to Postcolonial Literatures of Liberation* (New York: Columbia University Press, 2003).

DIARY OF A BOTANIST

1

Alone with a stalk of celery I squat to urinate on a mound of parsley. I walk into a forest that glows in darkness. I lift the wings of a rainbow lorikeet and stroke its green veins. Its eyes thick as clouds see me as purple eucalyptus. *Who are you and why have you come?* I kiss. My tongue whirls around its orange gum. It shivers with joy. I sweat. More pine needles to count. Inside the laboratory I wash, rinse, blot dry this year's shoot cut from pine trees and store it in plastic bags at 4 degrees. *Everything must be stored in plastic.* One needle per stalk is infected with fungi. I mark the infection with ink. *All infections must be marked.* In the evenings, kookaburras come looking for diced meat. They laugh at my armpits, my soap-dried hands. They see me sway, sweat, smell my own tongue. *Here, there. Here, there.* They laugh at my hair. I follow their rusted wings. Tell me where I should urinate.

2

Came from, and why? Right, while its pale tongue licked my finger, the beak tweaked to the left, tweaked. Close my eyes and lay my head on the track. The pages of my diary, a runaway train. The parrot's shiny again. *Here, there.* I knit with your hair, for my veins are delicate. Will you come to me? My departure is delayed. Blood is never secure. The diseased encountered a parrot, a rainbow lorikeet. It's I. Yes, like a dull mirror with blotches of rust. Ail! Trying to remember home, where I tacked next to other bags in the fridge. My experiment is done. Pine needles have been stained and bagged. Yes, needles can spill out. So bag them, bag.

3

I will tell you what the parrot said to me. I will tell you botanist, a botanist, the botanist. She lives in a forest. Eucalyptus leaves never rot. How sane. Her tongue, bagged in plastic, splits. Arrived insane, she scrubs kitchen counters, cutting boards, knives, the edges of a dish rack. She scrubs the fridge daily. The door stays wet. I will tell you she urinates here, there as instructed. She follows me, for needles pierce. A, an, the. She prefers nothing. I will tell you how she repeats to herself in a forest. *Which way? Which way?* I will tell you how sane she stays insane in a forest. She never fucks. *This is a pen. This is an apple. Hello. Goodbye. I have black eyes. I have black hair.* She is botanist. She is a botanist. She is the botanist. She cannot laugh. She cannot leave.

4

In the forest since 1981. My nationality. My nation. I am not saying. I am not staying. I am not sane. I am not same. I am not Chinese. I am not Japanese. I speak English. I speak. Mother lives in a house. I store infected pine needles behind the door, the thick clouds. Inside the laboratory, I count again. I was ten. I was sad. I don't remember. *Who let the engine run? Who ordered cyanide?* I only scream at night. I have dreams. My port of arrival. I defy the cradle law like an unwed parrot. No one is alarmed. After the experiment, I wipe. Mother has mishandled meat again. Bitch. The door has to be wiped again. Yes, I hope to die. Pine needles fall like hair. Yes, I bag everything. Fungi can grow. There are also pine trees in my country. No one knows how to symbolize home. The clouds, the fog, I was sad. I delay sameness. I delay you. I hope to marry you, you, and you. I hope to marry your nation.

FROM NOON—
TO ALL SURVIVING
BUTTERFLIES

1

The neocolonizers will soon perish. A farce is a farce, but the bombs fall anyway. Craters are formed and war correspondents travel in moonlight. The impression of traveling on the moon is born. Blood flows beneath ash. Dummies drop from the sky. A farce is a farce, B-29s never land. No mention is made of imperialism as a logical phase of capitalism. An old peasant stays behind to save his house, his son's legacy—his written Chinese in ink and brush. He runs along the crooked ditches of rice paddies, misses his footing. An aerial view reveals that he's a gook in white pajamas, normal for the daytime.

2

I belong to none except the gone. I keep a leaded poison in my pocket. I wish to perish before I die. Perhaps I was 19 or 20. I posed with the head of photography of Donga Daily. At dusk, I took a photo of the oldest living person south of the border. He was a farmer and smoked daily. June 1950, I took a sticky poison from the photo lab. I showed my hands to the soldiers from the North. Too soft, they said and let me go. I hid in the attic of an empty house, Father's house. He sold my camera for a sack of rice—he never worked a day in his life. I wish to perish before I die. I read fiction in Korean and Japanese. Yi Sang was my favorite. I listened to the radio. Americans are coming. I drank water and ate salt. The poison reached the socket of my eye.

3

The extent of loss is unknown. The text has been lost beyond the cuts. Father's documents have been rolled, tied together in string I made from hemp in winter under a lit pine nut oil. Grandfather carefully wrapped the documents in cloth and buried them under the house. Has Human Nature gone—unknowing of his dread abode—Fragments of my journey to the end of a nation. I arrived alone in a white top and long skirt with a sack, wearing thinly padded cotton socks and pointed rubber shoes. A normal view shows gooks' women fluttering about. Some had children on their backs. I was never taught to read as a girl. A normal document is not rolled but folded in half, then scissored. The cuts are jagged or straight. I will teach my daughters how to read the extent of the end.

4

Leave Him. Abort Him. Could you? Tell Him—my tenses are wrong on purpose. There is no need for pronouns, for I have abandoned them all. I take back all I said of Nation's stigma. Master's language is no home for a shoeless bee. Nation's regret is universal like the margins of none. Leave Her. Abort Her. You did. Tell Her—my ankles are swollen without Him. The great pronoun has been assassinated. Should I leave? I could return to my tenses, my distant wings. My loss neatly folded, wiped, and laminated to repel dust. A land of mourning is where I belong. Tell Him—she is not dead. She signifies without me. Leave Them. And go where? Master's language is forever thoughtful about what happened before something. Happy language! Shame is attached to syntax. Seal it or numb it. Most terrible pain you can imagine. Ask *OED*! In my house, the shoed are put to sleep and the shoeless forever depart. Going to dooms of napalm! Going to Guantanamo!

Notes on FROM NOON

"From noon" and "to all surviving Butterflies" are originally separate phrases. They were taken from the facsimile of Emily Dickinson's manuscript in *Bolts of Melody*, edited by Mabel Loomis Todd and Millicent Todd Bingham (Harper & Brothers Publishers, 1945)

"No mention is made of imperialism as a logical phase of capitalism" is from *How Europe Underdeveloped Africa* by Walter Rodney (Howard University Press, 1982).

"Has Human Nature gone—unknowing of his dread abode—" is from *Radical Scatters: Emily Dickinson's Fragments and Related Texts*, 1870-1886, edited by Marta L. Werner (University of Michigan Press, 1999).

TWIN FLOWER, MASTER, EMILY

1 DEAR TWIN FLOWER,

Only—true men—survive. Prior to military pornography, one never thought about petroleum byproducts. Tarzon bomb—a thing of the past—forgiven and forgotten. Daisy Cutter—lags! Consent is everywhere—Geography—Eternity! Terminate the notion of class when carrying out simulated bombing runs. Division is threadlike—scallop-toothed—a pretense of some kind—willed arbitrarily. It takes approximately twenty minutes to cut the waist of a Third World nation. Excellent yet inferior—this is why—we bang-bang in the woods. It is every man's dearest wish.

Yours, Master

2 DEAR EMILY,
·····················

For poetry—I have you. One need not be a House—One need not be a Nation or a Master for that matter. Delicate and beautiful, common in rich mossy woods, in pairs, we live. We are crimson-pink, particularly in the mountains. The rough terrain is not visible to many, but somewhat green and fatigued, demilitarized! A nod from far away is hollow. True men—How shall I greet them? Nation building is kind and generous. It is common to decline it. Emily, Shall I—bloom?

Yours, Twin Flower

3 DEAR TWIN FLOWER,

Your sister left me—she was cheerful—though maddened—knows the doings of Master. In fact—she lives it! Regretfully small and anxious—frequently far from home—Do stay! I am so near myself— Your sister is too. Near—Far—how was it arranged? Suicide is not an option—perhaps Resistance. Send me a portrait of your Distance! For politics—I have Walter—white racism which came to pervade the world was an integral part of capitalist mode of production.

Yours, Emily

4 DEAR MASTER,

I do! Autogeography, I do! Deeply lobed, in defiance of pretentious form, I push a petal from my Gown. An orator, born from jets, never met a translator. Orator, map out a wasteland between the front and the Chinese border. Such is—neocoloniality. I do! Autotranslation, I do! History can confront napalm. Sister's madness is as good as mine. We make the biggest picture in the world. Shallow and spiked, nodding in air, we endure barbed wire. Daisy Cutter can touch us, cut us, demolish our petals. Our gown can stain like a drape. Translator for hire! Hire me. See you at DMZ!

Yours, Twin Flower

....

"We bang-bang in the woods" was reported by a New York Times reporter in 1950, the first year of the Korean War. A South Korean policeman was about to execute forty civilians who were supposedly communists. The quote is from Bruce Cumings' *Korea's Place in the Sun* (W.W. Norton & Company, 1997).

"One need not be a house," "I push a petal from my Gown," and "Shall I—bloom?" are from Thomas H. Johnson's *Final Harvest: Emily Dickinson* (Little, Brown and Company, 1962).

"White racism which came to pervade the world was an integral part of capitalist mode of production" is from *How Europe Underdeveloped Africa* by Walter Rodney (Howard University Press, 1982).

A JOURNEY FROM NEOCOLONY TO COLONY

She went to Hong Kong in 1972. She was ten and knew only Korean then. She imagined there were two of her. She imagined me. I grew up in South Korea while she grew up in Hong Kong. I stay where I am.

My message to you:
I was left behind. Home is in layers.

Your message to me:
Green tea is the norm and nothing is added. In the Colony's economy it is essential that every opportunity should be taken to make one-self known. If you are from an unknown neocolony, you are nothing and will duly remain so until the date of your departure. Take a sip and stay close to family members. Your luggage will soon absorb the fog. The ferry you are on is in for a surprise—Tea and the English. It is now evident that the Colony can hope to support its greatly swollen population on a reasonable standard of living. Your language is optional. It is ideal for your new domestic arena: a three-bedroom flat and a balcony big enough to hold you and your sadness. We all appreciate the view of the harbor. Do not search for trees or blossoms. The sparrows will stop chirping after dusk. Do not let your coat weigh you down. There is no winter here. Of course, you may be low. That is the Law. Setting up house in the Colony usually involves relative safety and uncertainty. Have another sip. Green tea is the norm and nothing is added. Do not let the absence of curfew go to

your head. We realize the distance is overwhelming. That is an essential aspect of the Colony. If you are from an unknown neocolony, it is not necessary to identify yourself. We are not interested. We appreciate rapid growth.

My message to you:

Home is in layers. I live as if you had never left. I live in the house you were born in and speak your optional language. Here it is winter. I wear your scarf with ribbons and red mittens. I think of you as a child. Your have a view of the harbor and I have a view of the river. The distance is overwhelming. There has been a change in the Law. The 1961 Law is reinforced by the 1972 Law. What follows the Law? We are low. Your mother sent the suitcase of used clothes. I wear your sleeveless dresses and smell your fog. My sparrows have no place to go. I don't know if my clouds reach you or not. I think of you as a child. I wait for your return.

Your message to me:

I know homesickness. It is imaginable and involves collectivity to some degree. It begins with a family in the distance. Safety is nothing. Departure is nothing. Colony is something but neocolony is nothing. Winter is nothing, yet the Law is something. Ultimately, you are low. Ideology exists in layers. The Colonial is spatial. A descriptive theory, if you will. Dinner, the main meal of the day, originally taken at noon, had gradually been getting later, until in the 18th century it would fall between 3 or 4 in the afternoon. In the early evening came the tea hour, the polite visiting time. Your family may feel awkward at a table. You are now separated by chairs. You now sleep high above the floor under the removable sheets. You dream in layers: the mountain, the sea, the river, the bridge, and the ferry overlap, fold, then depart. Your optional language is likely to deform. Your mother may develop a disorder—the price of the inner world. Take your shoes off when you enter the house, but it is not appropriate to do so in front of the Law. Home is nothing and so are you. Clouds fade over time. You must endure the distance. The fog is your home.

My message to you:
You are gone. Please come. I have your comb. I know homesickness. It unfolds like Mother's umbrella. I dress your paper dolls, the penciled closet. I pace the bridge, your hair pin in my hair. The river is muddy. I unfold my arms and take off my shoes. I am none. Please come. I have your comb. Be low. Be no. Say no to dinner and fog.

Your message to me:
Forgetting is lovely and Father's well is bottomless. Freud says: *the way in which national tradition and the individual's childhood memories are formed might turn out to be entirely analogous.*

Indeed, a higher authority can shift the aim of the resistance to memory. Madness may be a form of resistance. Forgetting is lovely and Father's well is bottomless. In order to remember an incident painful to national feeling, a lower psychic agency must resist the higher authority. However, it is against the Law. Tea and false memories. Which is lovelier? Colony or neocolony? The shift in the aim is minor. Forget something then remember something else. The loveliest of all is the unconscious—it is lively. In defense of nation's paramnesia, tea must be served at all times. Migration, my nation! The family in the distance must be oceans apart. Closeness may lead to nationalism. Follow orderly obsessions. Wash and clean when in doubt. Scrub the edges of your memory. Childhood loneliness can shift its aim. Nation's loneliness is false category. Be fraud. Be Law.

My message to you:
Are you sad? I am not mad. You sat on Father's lap. 1972 was the year of your departure. I remember your flowered shirt and shorts, a hair pin in your hair. Law was becoming and you were leaving. My clouds followed you. Are you lovely? I am lively. My sparrows fly at night across the ocean and remember your flowers. I am not fallow. I follow.

Notes on A JOURNEY

································

Sigmund Freud's quote is from *Forgetting Things* (Penguin, 2005).

DIARY OF A TRANSLATOR

1

A system without translation is called I-no-system. While MSG, a natural seasoning derived from soybeans, attempts to become the moon, a child nibbles on green onions. Not yet, not yet, shouted I-no-system. The skin of translation, neither pink nor grey, stared at the clock of theory. Nothing happened to MSG, and I-no-system cradled the child into oblivion. Therefore, the moon remained as the moon.

2

As the child grew, the moon waned. I-no-system nibbled on green onions and became suicidal. MSG, the clock, and the skin were strictly carnivorous and plotted a denial of home. MSG fell into a temporary melancholia. What theory? the clock chimed every hour. And the skin became anti-itself. Lips of home amassed internally. Cyanide smells like almonds, shouted I-no-system. The child drifted from nation to nation. The moon arose distance after distance.

3

Loneliness is a fine thing, said the clock. The child had no reply. The moon replied instead. What is truly fine? The stars around me, galaxies of them, mute lumps of darkness. I-no-system, who will translate you? Childless and empty like madness. I-no-system used a plastic shovel to scoop up the lips above, pretending to be sane and homesick. I shall return! it declared. Finally the child spoke. What is truly home? I am here but I remember there.

4

I am always here, said MSG. "And I am the most celebrated image of home. Have me, be like me. Without theory, without the moon. Forget home. Here is plentiful. It was one in the morning. What cyanide? chimed the clock. I-no-system decided on carbon monoxide instead. It was odorless. It was not televised. It was documented by the unknown lips. The moon wept behind the cloud. The child said to the stars: Detachment is painful, so is madness. Home is a system of longing, and suicide is a system of exile. Neither is bloodless.

5

The clock had a different response: The clock is mad. Who's mad? The clock is mad. Decolonize madness! Speak English! Only nation! Translation is occupied. Who is colonial? Mad, mad, mad! It is one in the morning. The clock is mad. Did I say theorize or colonize? It is one in the morning. Let the moon piss by itself. Undo madness. Undo English. Mad, mad, mad! Colonial madness, you translate supreme.   It is one in the morning. Dick talk, dick talk. No, English only! Nation only! Do you speak English? Thank you. The clock is mad. Thank you. It is one in the morning. Thank you. Theorize me, colonize me. Thank you. The clock is mad. Dear Father, Dear Mother, Dear English speaking Ladies and Gentlemen.

6

In winter the child's mother took a taxi to the peak of the mountain. She looked for camellia blossoms while the child dreamt in English. Sparrows chirped loudly outside the tall apartment building. Why do sparrows cry? asked the child. Mother replied, They always cry before sleep. In winter the child cleaned windows for Mother with crumpled South China Morning Post and Windex. The less humid air made the child homesick. In school the child read Auden and Eliot, then failed O level English. In another school across the Pacific Ocean, the child listened to Paz, Milosz, Brodsky, Sarton, Levertov. Read Emily the most. Across the ocean, sparrows looked for camellias to sleep on, but they only found prickly sage. In winter sparrows cried.

7

Talk egg! chimed the clock. Time to wake up from dreams and sparrows! I am already translated, said MSG as it awoke. Egg off! clock replied. Egg did talk egg talk. Talk egg! chimed the clock. Egg did. Long time ago, the moon laid an egg, which became an occupied egg, war egg, then a neo-occupied egg. The moon's egg was a doubled egg. Egg and egg, a divided egg. History and memory fed egg. Not a hollow egg. Not a nation's egg. Egg did talk egg talk! Egg did. Egg off! Empire must go!

WEAVER IN EXILE

1

Father, moon is full. I'm weaving. Steamed carp with lotus roots, how was it? Was its tongue as tender as a cow's? How you love rolling cooked eyes with your teeth as if you were scraping meat off two bulging stars. I'm out of bark, threads, and hair. I'm weaving paper with falling shit from stars.

You ignore black holes that crush turtle shells into fine sand. You ignore my loom twisted like wisteria trunks from my copious tears. Stars are separate. I want to be a dead star.

Herder easily forgets me. He's an addict. He writes love songs about how there must be parting. His ox stinks. I left him for a comet.

On July 7th, I'll tie prayers to crows and magpies' feet and pee. Father, expect rain. I'll pose briefly by the bridge. Come ready with your camera.

2

Stars are whores.

I weave pubic hair for dolls and frogs naively lit by your orange lamps. If cloth is meat, what is blood? Try weaving shredded wrists, decapitated hearts. Was my mother a sacred bitch?

The earthen bridge takes me to a shallow creek. Is this the Milky Way? Babies or children on bridges annoy me. Who separates them from mothers? You? A galaxy of moss. I'm tired of this imitation sky.

Let's skip to your dream. How many lamps did you see? Do you re- member east and west? Explain the island. Why is the bridge flat? Describe the distance between the murmuring pines. Did you love my mother? Will I remarry?

3

Loneliness is a dense thing. There's no data inside a collapsed star. My tongue glides into a ring of silence. My heart beats in practical terms. There is no moon, no cycle, no time. X-rayed a thousand times, my sex is neutered. What cooks inside are sulphur, calcium, and iron—the stuff from blood and bones, the stuff from fermenting stars. Let's not say loneliness is solitude, for distance is not marriage.

Ask the butterflies. Prostitutes can only marry GIs.

I would explode if a hot fetus pressed against my belly. Sometimes baby breaths can cause nausea. I remember mother as a river beyond reach. I saw her only at night. Her milk was white. Her breasts had hair like peaches. There were no gaps in her caress. I looked like a boy, so I attempted to swallow her nipples. Next night, she returned with tar smeared on her breasts. I never saw her again.

Detachment is easy. I thought the Herder could point me to the Milky Way. Instead he drank his head off while chasing his ox. Father, I think you are a closet weaver. Murmuring pines have told me so. They say you can't measure distance like me and you never drink. Distance is always far like tarred breasts. What use are lit lamps, when we are both blind to blackness?

4

You lug buckets of shit from one pond to another. Babies fall out of wombs like ducks from Venus. When do tears split into water and salt? The universe is one vast puddle of moss with pink poker dots. One less duck won't stop Herder from hugging his beer bottle smeared in ox shit. Don't be fooled by chaos of crows, they're just messing with sonic waves. The universe isn't as deep as you think. However, milk is deep. I forget babies. I forget to change their diapers. Like cheese, they curdle on their own. I held one and felt I could love anything. Mine had a cyst too heavy for his forehead. To feed him, I had to hold a needle between my nipple and his mouth. I learned that even milk needs distance.

You sent me to the west where the moon is always a sliver from the shadow of deformity. My loom faces the east, screeching like a starved ox. I weave for mothers without sons. Carps, peppers, noses, and oversized genitals on fine silk pulled from the inner holes of caterpillars. My feet are raw from peddling sex. I wrap the cyst in newspaper and drop it in the starry river, while you pray to the pointless sky.

5

Dear Father, I am sitting on crows' backs that wobble with grease. Stars look like pebbles from here. Magpies scream with joy. I weep from solitude of claws.

6

Help me, She-bear, help me help me. Father flung me to the core of soot. My tears are turbulent from its pulsing thumb. Nebula has nice ring.

7

Dear rock,

Dear tree,

Dear sky,

Please let Father die.

From the braids of crows' backs I open a door. Drops of white resin lead to a pond of molten carps. Flimsy orange and blue skin swim across the Milky Way, leaving nothing behind.

Dear rock,

Dear tree,

Dear Father,

Please let me cross.

Notes on WEAVER IN EXILE

"Weaver in Exile" is based on a Korean folktale called "Kyŏnu wa jiknyŏ" (Herder and Weaver).

PETITE MANIFESTO

THE FIRST HOUSE
....

I should have died, but I clung onto my mother's uterus, my first house, as she rode on the bus back home. I begin at the bottom of the cold water, inside the first house *where meaning hops into the spacey emptiness between two named historical languages.*

I end up elsewhere and lie in bed all day. Bored and lonely, I'm likely to die. It is likely that my mother said something to me during her early stage of pregnancy: *the relationship between social logic, social reasonableness, and the disruptiveness of figuration in social practice.*

I begin at the bottom, petite and all. Logic is glorious, so a decision must be made about translation. It's premature: translation must remain as ordinary as the bed, where I'm likely to die.

MIRRORS AGAINST LOGIC
....

Detached, are you? Cross the river as an act of political resistance. The bridge has been bombed, walk across the floating bridge. I wish and wish in bed. *I open a mirror and enter, mother is inside a mirror, sitting.* I wish and wish for a husband. *I open a mirror and enter again, grandmother is inside a mirror, sitting.* I know that a poem must *enter, and enter again.* Yet, I wish and wish for him to arrive. The spacey emptiness between the mirrors, between the sheets, will agree with nothing, resemble nothing. I wish and wish for a petition.

THE ACCUMULATED SPEECH

What is the accumulated speech of the mothers? You may reassemble the sheets. Mattress upon mattress, peas against peas, petite in their own right, save me, take me, marry me, and despite such acute misappropriation of the Third World literature, strung together in the context of disenchanted accessibility, only to fail miserably elsewhere in English, as ordinary as the bed, you are likely to die, and, in fact, why didn't you? before you encountered the grammar of "This translation is mine" and cross the river, as detached as the peas in a pod, the string of pearls, the pregnant mothers, the ripples of fingernails, then the problem becomes clear, *we are dealing with a strategy of immediacy, a local liberation.*

Notes on PETITE MANIFESTO

······································

"where the meaning hops..." Gayatri Chakravorty Spivak, *Outside in the Teaching Machine*, (New York & London, Routledge, 1993).

"I open a mirror and enter..." Kim Hyesoon, *Anxiety of Words: Contemporary Poetry by Korean Women*, trans. Don Mee Choi (Zephyr Press, 2006).

"we are dealing with a strategy..." Frantz Fanon, *The Wretched of the Earth*, trans. Constance Farrington (New York, Grove Press, 1963).

Acknowledgements

Many thanks to the editors of the journals in which some of these poems have previously appeared: *Action Yes, Cipher, Fairytale Review, Feminist Studies, Fence, La Petite Zine,* and *Tinfish.*

I didn't envision a book of my own poems until the Action Books editors, Joyelle and Johannes, appeared in my life and told me to keep writing. I am also grateful to Deborah Woodard as I wrote many of the poems in her classes. This book is dedicated to Jay.

About the Author

Don Mee Choi was born in South Korea and came to the U.S. via Hong Kong. She is a translator of contemporary Korean women's poetry; her translation titles include *When the Plug Gets Unplugged* (Tinfish, 2005), *Anxiety of Words: Contemporary Poetry by Korean Women* (Zephyr, 2006), and *Mommy Must Be a Fountain of Feathers* (Action Books, 2008). She lives and works in Seattle.

About the Cover

In order to create the horizontal stripes seen on the cover, the designer inserted lines of *To All Boys and Men!* into the JPEG code of a photograph of a chrysanthemum, thus distorting the image.